RAISING THE ROOF!

A TEMPLAR BOOK

This edition published in the UK in 2025 by Templar Books.
First published in the UK in 2024
by Templar Books, an imprint of Bonnier Books UK
5th Floor, HYLO, 105 Bunhill Row, London, EC1Y 8LZ
The authorised representative in the EEA
is Bonnier Books UK (Ireland) Limited.
Registered office address: Floor 3, Block 3,
Miesian Plaza Dublin 2, D02 Y754, Ireland
compliance@bonnierbooks.ie
www.bonnierbooks.co.uk

ISBN 978-1-83587-329-8

Edited by Carly Blake and Sophie Hallam
Designed by Ted Jennings
Production by Neil Randles

Printed in China

MIX
Paper | Supporting
responsible forestry
FSC® C104723
FSC
www.fsc.org

To Mum and Dad, for supporting, putting up with and believing in Captain Foghorn. Behind every sound is an unsung hero. You don't know how much you have done – J.P.

To Valeria, thanks for the constant support and guidance – M.B.

Jack Pepper is one of the UK's youngest commissioned composers and youngest-ever national radio presenters. In his teens, he wrote for the Royal Opera House, Classic FM, Royal Liverpool Philharmonic Orchestra, Bournemouth Symphony Orchestra and the Band of HM Royal Marines, alongside pop, jazz and theatre work that saw his music nominated for a Canadian JUNO Award and performed everywhere from the Royal Albert Hall to the Roundhouse. He has presented for Magic Radio's Magic Classical (formerly Scala Radio) and Magic at the Musicals, and hosts both the musical theatre and classical shows for British Airways.

Michele Bruttomesso Born and raised in Vicenza, Italy, Michele Bruttomesso is an illustrator that consistently brings a touch of joy to every project he works on. A great punk rock music fan, he came to prominence while still in art school by drawing album reviews for local bands. He has illustrated for magazines, children's books, board games, posters and animation. He's the author of Drengexplosion (2019), an experimental webcomic that mixes cartoon and animation.

RAISING THE ROOF!

Written by
Jack Pepper

Illustrated by
Michele Bruttomesso

templar
books

CONTENTS

20 CLASSICAL ROCKSTARS

MY WORLD OF MUSIC

I'm Jack Pepper. I'm a composer, which means I write music!
I'm here to introduce you to a world of classical sounds.
There's never been a dull moment in this musical history – so be
prepared for colourful characters that will intrigue you, music
that will astound you and stories that will inspire you.
This is my story...

Dots on Paper...

When I was six, I loved singing hymns in school but spent more
time watching the teacher play the piano. I soon realised that
what I'd been singing corresponded to the dots on the sheet
music and the piano keys under her fingertips. I started to
learn the piano, and made up my own tunes...

James Bond

On holidays, I'd listen to the James Bond film theme
songs on a loop. I was fascinated by the way they
featured a full orchestra (see page 16), using a range
of instruments to such effect that I came to think of
the various instruments as like different colours in a
painting. I loved how these songs told stories, too;
they were like three-minute mini-dramas!

My First Orchestra

When I was 16, London's Royal Opera House ran a
competition inviting young composers to write and
record a short piece, called a fanfare (a short piece of
music designed as a call to attention or a celebration).
I sent a short fanfare for four instruments... and was
amazed to be selected! This led to working with a
60-person orchestra and a famous conductor.

Classic FM

After that, I was asked to write the 25th birthday music for UK
radio station Classic FM. My music was played on the radio,
and I was also interviewed about my work. One of the team
suggested that I should consider presenting, as I enjoyed telling
stories about the music. I began to consider a career in radio,
and not just writing music...

Pop Songs

I decided not to study at university and went straight into the world of work when I was 18. Soon, I was writing pop songs in Los Angeles, USA, and writing for different orchestras in the UK. I definitely would not have been able to do this without some incredible mentors around me!

Scala Radio

When I was 19, a new classical music station was launched in the UK: Scala Radio. I presented the weekly arts show. Presenting on the radio not only allowed me to listen to a wide range of music and share my own musical discoveries, but the interviews let me meet my idols and learn from them too!

Musicals

My love of storytelling in orchestral pieces and on radio led me to musical theatre. From the age of 20, I started writing original stories through song. My first show, *Duet*, tells the real-life story of my piano teacher: the neighbour who inspired my teenage self to spread my musical wings.

A Composer's Life

As a composer, it can be hard to switch the music off, as you always have something sounding in your brain. Songwriter Burt Bacharach had problems sleeping, as he always had music in his head. Some composers, such as George Gershwin and Claude Debussy, worked best at night but others, such as Benjamin Britten and Pyotr Tchaikovsky, preferred to write in the morning. Composing is a job and a craft like sculpting: you have your stone, and then you need to chip away and carve out a recognisable structure.

WHAT IS CLASSICAL MUSIC?

So what even *is* classical music? Its history stretches back more than a thousand years. Classical music represents so many different faces, places, eras and experiences: it is a living and ever-evolving diary of people and the times they live in. That means – whether you've lived with classical music for decades or if you're dipping in for the first time – there's always more to discover.

PERSIAN CLASSICAL MUSIC
Known for the dastgah system (a traditional framework of melodies), with instruments like the tar and setar.

KOREAN CLASSICAL MUSIC
Known for its court and folk traditions, with instruments like the gayageum and ajaeng.

Global Music

Classical music is truly global. So when using this label, let's be more geographically specific – for example, 'Western classical tradition' often includes European and American musicians, but there are many other classical traditions around the world. Ever since the late 1800s, the Western tradition became ever-more directly influenced by 'world' traditions. For example, gamelan (a traditional Indonesian percussion orchestra) came to exhibitions in Europe, and Western composers soon incorporated these sounds into their own music. While this book aims to take us to many different places, faces and ideas, we're largely exploring the 'Western classical tradition'. But as we'll see, music always has been and always will be a cultural melting pot...

AFRICAN CLASSICAL MUSIC
Rhythm is key, with many interweaving rhythmic lines. Imagine five people all clapping a different pattern, simultaneously; this is called polyrhythm.

INDIAN CLASSICAL MUSIC
Two major branches: Hindustani (North Indian) and Carnatic (South Indian). It features intricate ragas (melodies) and talas (rhythms) played on instruments like sitar and tabla.

JAPANESE CLASSICAL MUSIC

Court music and religious Buddhist chant feature in this tradition, with instruments like the koto and shamisen.

CHINESE CLASSICAL MUSIC

Many regional styles such as Beijing opera, and silk and bamboo ensembles. Features traditional instruments such as the guqin and pipa.

INDONESIAN CLASSICAL MUSIC

Traditional music includes gamelan featuring gongs and other percussion instruments.

MIDDLE EASTERN CLASSICAL MUSIC

Known for its virtuoso singers, performing long melismas (singing many different notes/pitches for one syllable or sound).

LATIN AMERICAN CLASSICAL MUSIC

A range of styles, including Brazilian choro (instrumental music with influences from Africa, Europe and Indigenous Brazil) and Argentine tango (dance style and genre of music).

Changing Perspectives

Even in the 'Western' tradition, our understanding of 'classical' is constantly evolving. There are many composers who lived centuries ago but who are only just being rediscovered. There's also something darker to this. History is written by those in control – and frequently that's white, privileged men. Many women and Black musicians were composing, but have not been as well documented in history books. In some cases their works were performed regularly in their lifetime, but their pieces were not published – meaning their music only lasted as long as they did. This is because, before computers, every music piece had to be written (and copied) out by hand. If you lost the sheets, you lost the piece. Thankfully, we're now rediscovering many amazing composers.

Lost in Music

So, you'll see that 'classical' can mean a lot of things. Together, we'll explore some key words and areas in Western classical music, and then some colourful characters who have made it over the years – each providing a different definition of the word 'classical'. So pick a page, dive in... and see where it leads!

♪ LISTEN!

As you read through the pages, look out for this symbol for songs to listen to. These make up a playlist that I've especially selected to tell the story of Western classical music over the centuries. Search for each song online and create your own personal playlist. See page 76 for streaming platforms.

11

A MUSICAL HISTORY

The history of Western classical music can be divided into different eras: blocks of time where music was written in a certain style. Here's a whistlestop tour...

Early Music
c. 500–1400

For centuries, music was an oral tradition: tunes were taught by word of mouth. The Roman Catholic Church started to formalise and keep records of music in the Middle Ages. Featuring heavily were religious chants – vocal music that was often monophonic (a single melodic line or voice without any accompanying music).

♪ *Misa de Septuagesima* sung by the Saint Pierre de Solesmes Abbey Monks' Choir. The Choir is one of the world's most renowned ensembles specialising in monophonic Gregorian chant music.

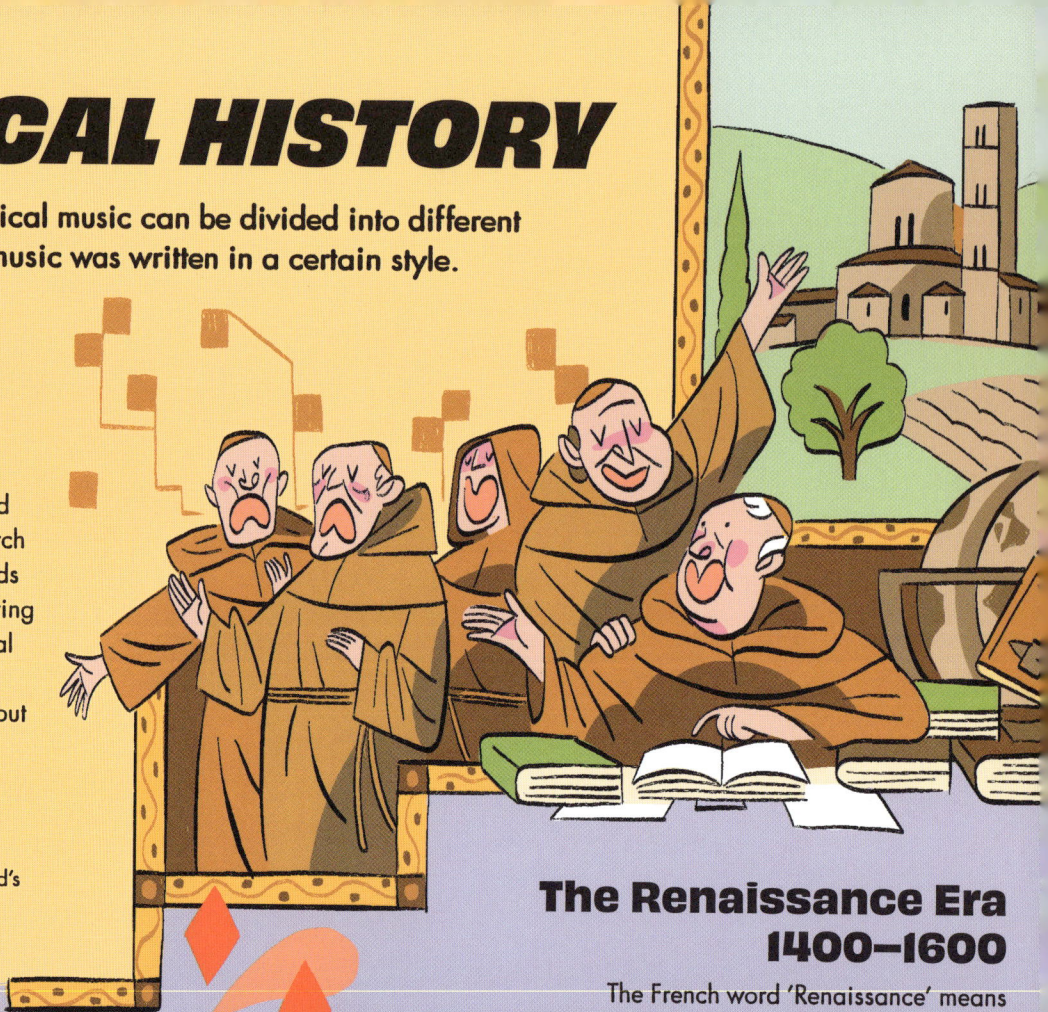

The Renaissance Era
1400–1600

The French word 'Renaissance' means 'rebirth', and this era saw great advancements in science, technology, philosophy and the arts, including music. In contrast to the Middle Ages, music became increasingly polyphonic (different melodies or voices playing or singing at the same time, creating a web of interweaving sound).

♪ Thomas Tallis (1505–1585) wrote choral music for English monarchs. Listen to *Spem In Alium*, an epic piece with 40 different voice parts!

The Baroque Era
1600–1750

Baroque music is highly decorative, with elaborate melodies and dense polyphonic textures. The period saw the birth of opera (see page 22) and a boom in music for solo instruments, like the harpsichord.

♪ Antonio Vivaldi (1678–1741) was a virtuoso violinist, priest and teacher at an orphanage. Despite composing over 800 pieces of music, he was only recognised as a classical musician 300 years after his death! Listen to *The Four Seasons* – musical pictures of different times of year.

The Classical Era
1750–1825

Reacting against the excesses of the Baroque era, music was all about a clean, pure sound, with less cluttered textures and singing melodies. Composers started to emphasise emotion and feeling as key qualities in music, instead of grand structures and forms.

♪ Carl Philipp Emanuel Bach (1714–1788) pioneered a 'sensitive style' that featured stark contrasts in mood and volume. Listen to his keyboard sonatas.

The Romantic Era
1825–1900

Romanticism is all about the power of the individual. Composers began writing from a more personal point of view, with strong emotion and vivid storytelling. They became stars and 'masters', respected and glorified. Music became longer and more adventurous. The orchestra became larger – and louder – as new instruments and technologies were developed.

♪ Louise Farrenc (1804–1875) fought for equal pay for women at the Paris Conservatoire (music school), where she was the first female professor of piano. Farrenc wrote courageous symphonies that were full of passion, like her. Listen to Symphony no. 3 in G minor.

The Twentieth Century
1900–2000

This is when the musical rulebook went out the window! Aeroplane propellers and sirens sometimes appeared in the orchestra, and new technology began to be incorporated into pieces. Music became more dissonant (clashing), and there really was no 'standard' or expectation.

♪ Margaret Bonds (1913–1972) was an American composer of theatre works, popular songs and classical pieces on social themes, including one inspired by civil rights leader Martin Luther King. Listen to *Troubled Water*.

Contemporary
2000–Present

Anything goes! Minimalist pieces draw on the repetitive patterns of pop, while avant-garde music experiments with clashing sounds. Contemporary classical music blurs lines between genres like rock, jazz and pop. Performances take place in unexpected locations away from the concert hall, including car parks and train stations.

♪ Errollyn Wallen's (1958–present) music breaks down barriers between genres. She has also written operas exploring the Black experience. Listen to *Horseplay: Lively*.

THE INGREDIENTS OF SOUND

What is music made of? As a composer, I have lots of different ingredients I can include to make my musical dish. Music can be broken down, just like a recipe, into parts that work together to make a piece whole – so let's tuck in and see what music is made of...

NOTES

Every individual sound you hear with a specific pitch is a 'note'. On a page of sheet music, these are represented by dots of different shapes. Western classical music is a tradition that is written down – notated – in contrast to something like jazz, which is based on improvisation (making up your own notes as you play).

C D E F G A B C

PITCH

How high or low a note is. Music can be broken down into scales (notes next to each other that climb up or down). Nearly every note is associated with a letter from the alphabet. A, B, C, D, E, F and G represent specific pitches, and they occur in cycles, from lower to higher. Perfect pitch is the ability to hear a note and name the letter, without needing to play an instrument to check.

TEXTURE

The layers of a piece of music. Some pieces might spotlight a single instrument for a few moments: an exposed texture. Others might include a whole orchestra playing at the same time in an explosion of sound: a dense texture.

RHYTHM

The sequence of long and short notes, and the patterns these make together, is called rhythm. When we clap or we tap our feet, this is a rhythm.

TIMBRE

The character and quality of sound created by an instrument. A single instrument can have a wide variety of sounds. For example, a horn played at the bottom of its range sounds like an angry growl, but high up it can sound angelic.

TEMPO

The speed of a piece. Often indicated by a single Italian word like allegro (fast), andante (at a walking pace) or adagio (slow).

MELODY

The melody is the tune. As a piece unfolds, the original melody might be stretched or shortened, heard backwards or in a different rhythm, or played by another instrument.

LINE

Sheet music is like a map of a piece, telling us who plays what and when; on the page, each instrument has its own line.

RANGE

Instruments are categorised by how high or low they can play: a flute plays much higher notes than a bassoon (a bass instrument that plays much lower notes). Some instruments like the piano or violin have a very broad range with both high and low notes.

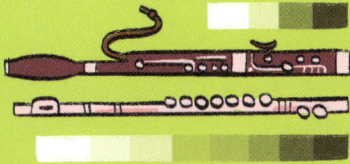

HARMONY

The sound made when multiple notes are played at the same time. These combinations of notes are called **chords**. These can be consonant (pleasant sounding, with the notes fitting together nicely) or dissonant (harsh sounding, where the notes clash).

DYNAMICS

Composers can specify changes in volume: this is called dynamics. Pieces often contrast a loud burst of notes with a quiet one. This creates a sense of contrast and dialogue.

pp p mp mf f ff

PHRASE

A sentence in music – it's made up of just a few musical notes.

MOVEMENT

A piece of music might be broken down into different movements, like the chapters of a novel. There are often three or four movements.

REGISTER

How high or low the music 'sits' for an instrument. If lots of the notes are very high, we'd call it a high 'register'.

Listen Out!

Consider all of these areas of music to listen out for in a piece and ways of describing what you hear; every work can be broken down into these key areas. Ask yourself: is this moment showing a thick or a thin texture? Is this harmony dissonant (clashing)? All these ingredients work together to make a piece distinct and emotive.

15

ORCHESTRA

An orchestra is a group of musicians playing together. It can be broken down into families: sub-sections of instruments that are played or made in a similar way. The families of the orchestra are strings, brass, woodwind and percussion, but other instruments such as piano, saxophone, drums or even a wind machine might also feature in more contemporary pieces.

In the 1600s and early 1700s, the orchestra was a small group of players, perhaps 20 or 30 people. As new instruments were invented, the orchestra became larger and louder. By the early 1800s, orchestras featured 60 or more players and a wider range of instruments. After the First World War (1914–1918), composers wrote for smaller orchestras as there was less money available to pay for larger groups. These are called chamber orchestras (see page 26), with similar instruments but generally no more than 50 players. Nowadays, symphony orchestras – 90 players or more – exist alongside these smaller groups.

Hector Berlioz's *Grande Messe des morts*

Hector Berlioz (1803–1869) included over 100 string players, 16 timpani (kettle drums) and four brass bands in this 1837 piece.

Orchestra Key:
From top to bottom

- Percussion
- Trumpets & Clarinets
- Trombones & Tubas
- Harp
- Grand Piano
- Horns
- Flutes & Piccolos
- Bassoons & Oboes
- Double Bass
- First Violins
- Second Violins
- Violas
- Cellos
- Conductor

Conductors

A conductor often leads the orchestra using hand movements (sometimes holding a baton, to make these gestures clearer) to keep everyone together, playing in time. Conductors also give cues to the players, reminding musicians when to start playing again (many instruments have long stretches without playing). The conductor also shapes the overall interpretation of a piece and decides what speed to play at.

Orchestras for All Abilities

The British Paraorchestra, created in 2012, is the world's first professional orchestra for both disabled and non-disabled players. Macbooks and iPads sit alongside traditional orchestral instruments, as well as brand-new devices. For example, Clarence Adoo, one of the UK's top trumpeters, had a car collision which left him paralysed. Now, he wears a specially made headset and blows into a tube which works with sensors controlling a mouse on a screen, channelling his breath to make a sound.

Types of Classical Music

As we saw in the history of musical eras, there are many different traditions and styles. The size and makeup of an orchestra can vary depending on the specific period. Indeed, the idea of a star conductor only really developed in the 1800s; before then, the first violinist often led the orchestra while playing alongside them. Before we meet the rockstars of classical music, let's explore some of these different areas.

SYMPHONY

The symphony has changed over the centuries, but it is essentially an extended piece of music for a large group of players. The word itself comes from the Greek, meaning 'sounding together'. It is often a composer's statement piece because the size and scale of the music make it hard to pull off.

A symphony is played by an orchestra, with tens or hundreds of people. There are lots of sections, called movements, each with their own tempo. It's like a painting on a huge canvas, or writing a novel with many characters and chapters. The opening movement is often loud and dramatic, while the second movement is slower and gentler. Movements provide contrast – with highs and lows, moments of tension and release, building to an ultimate finale.

LISTENING TIP

Keep your ears focused in the starting moments, as you can then trace how the original ideas are woven through the piece as it progresses.

🎵 Ludwig van Beethoven's Symphony no. 9, 4th movement

Never one to shy away from large orchestras, Ludwig van Beethoven (1770–1827) featured an entire choir (one of *the* first times human voices were included in a symphony). In the fourth movement, they sing 'Ode to Joy', a hymn celebrating togetherness among humanity.

1600s

The term 'symphony' is often used to refer to a large combination of instruments playing in various settings.

1700s

Orchestra music develops outside of the opera house. A three-movement structure is created, with a fast opening, a slow central section, and a fast ending.

1672

The first recorded public concert is held at composer John Banister's (c. 1625–1679) home in London, paving the way for public concerts in taverns and coffeehouses.

1748

The first building designed for public concerts is opened in Oxford, UK: the Holywell Music Room.

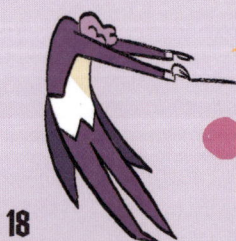

♪ Alice Mary Smith's Symphony no. 1 in C minor, 4th movement

The first known symphony written by a British woman, aged just 24, Alice Mary Smith (1839–1884) looks back towards the clarity and elegance of the 1700s, avoiding the emotion and excess that many writers of her time embraced.

♪ Amy Beach's 'Gaelic' Symphony in E minor, 2nd movement

An American prodigy who was writing music aged four, Amy Beach's (1867–1944) 'Gaelic' Symphony draws on traditional English, Scottish and Irish melodies.

♪ Philip Glass's *Heroes* and *Low*

Philip Glass (1937–present) is celebrated for bringing together different musical styles. With *Heroes* and *Low*, Glass wrote two symphonies inspired by albums from pop and mainstream music stars David Bowie and Brian Eno.

1775
London's first purpose-built concert hall opens: the Hanover Square Rooms.

1900s
Symphonies expand in scope, with single-movement and even ten-movement symphonies!

1800s
We start to see more programme music, pieces that tell specific stories. The orchestra gets bigger, and new instruments are invented.

Present
A symphony is an extended piece for orchestra. There is not a specific number of movements or instruments.

CONCERTO

A concerto is a large-scale piece of music for a soloist (a single person playing one instrument) and an orchestra. The soloist, playing anything from the violin to the trumpet, is positioned at the front of the orchestra, and plays against the backdrop of the wider group. A concerto puts a musical spotlight on a single instrument.

The concerto, like the symphony, is often made up of several movements, with different moods. But the concerto is also a conversation. The solo instrument 'talks' with the orchestra – a game of musical ping-pong, batting ideas back and forth and developing them as they go. Sometimes, this conversation becomes a battle, with the solo instrument fighting against the orchestra.

The ultimate chance for a soloist to show off is in what's called a cadenza. Towards the end of a movement, near the climax, the orchestra drops out, letting the soloist play entirely on their own. There are lots of fast notes, from the highest to the lowest and back. Many composers were talented soloists themselves: Edvard Grieg, Amy Beach and Wolfgang Amadeus Mozart all wrote their own piano concerti (the plural word for concerto) so they could star in their own concerts.

1700s

A concerto is increasingly a piece for one player, against the backdrop of a wider orchestra. Violins or keyboards are common solo instruments.

1600s

The first concerti are created in Italy by Alessandro Stradella (1643–1682) who divides the orchestra into the main ensemble (the *ripieno* or 'rest') and a smaller group of players (*concertino* meaning 'small ensemble').

Wolfgang Amadeus Mozart's Clarinet Concerto, 2nd movement

Wolfgang Amadeus Mozart (1756–1791) was one of the first composers to write for the clarinet. The clarinet had only recently been invented and had not been used widely as a solo instrument.

Edvard Grieg's Piano Concerto, 1st movement

This concerto has one of the most famous openings in classical music. Edvard Grieg (1843–1907) wrote it in 1868 shortly after the birth of his son. You can hear the joy and energy of youth in the music.

Jennifer Higdon's *Fly Forward*

Jennifer Higdon (1962–present) taught herself to play the flute aged 15 and started composing at 21. In 2010, she won the Pulitzer Prize for Music for this Violin Concerto, which is full of dazzling fast notes for the violinist to showcase their skills.

1900s–Present

The solo instrument is increasingly an unusual one, such as a double bass, trombone or a harmonica!

1800s

Players begin touring the world giving concerts. The concerto is a showcase for their skills, becoming longer and more complex.

21

OPERA

Opera is a story told through a combination of song, stage, sets, costumes and acting. Opera is highly collaborative – the composer writes the music (the score), the librettist pens the words, and a director then interprets the piece.

Opera is defined, musically, as being through-sung, meaning everything is sung, including every word of dialogue. The singers are often the stars. The Three Tenors (a tenor is a high male voice) became global megastars: Luciano Pavarotti, Placido Domingo and José Carreras. Their performance of 'Nessun Dorma', an aria from Giacomo Puccini's opera *Turandot* at the FIFA World Cup in 1990, was a worldwide sensation. Pavarotti later reached No. 2 in the UK Pop Singles Chart!

The earliest surviving opera comes from 1600, written by two Italian composers: Jacopo Peri and Giulio Caccini. Modern composers continue to write them, and the word continues to be interpreted broadly.

Key sections of music include:

Recitative – a speech-like song with lots of short notes and many words, telling us what's happening in the plot: the action.

Aria – the big songs for solo singers, showing a character reacting to events in the plot: the emotional heart of an opera.

Chorus – large numbers of singers performing together, commenting on the action. They're often used to represent groups of people, such as villagers, soldiers or fairies: the crowd.

1600s
Operas are performed for royal patrons and state events. The first public opera houses start to open.

1700s
Opera remains an entertainment for the wealthy. The music is often a showcase for the dazzling skills of the star singers.

Judith Weir's
King Harald's Saga 🎵

In 1979, Judith Weir (1954–present) wrote an opera for an unaccompanied soprano (high female voice) who sang eight different solo character roles, as well as another role that represented the entire Norwegian Army! The whole thing lasted just ten minutes…

Giacomo Puccini's 🎵
'Vissi d'arte' from Tosca

Set in Rome, Giacomo Puccini's (1858–1924) most famous opera is about a talented singer, Floria Tosca, who is in love with artist Mario Cavaradossi – which, like many of Puccini's operas, ends tragically. The aria 'Vissi d'arte' is sung by Floria shortly after she has killed Scarpia, a policeman, to save Mario. Puccini liked writing music late at night, while partying and playing cards with friends. For a composer who was celebrated for writing operas about real life – so-called *verismo* opera – it's appropriate he composed amid the hubbub of everyday living!

1800s

Operas are becoming huge spectacles, involving epic stage effects (like fake snow or live animals) and large props. The plots are dramatic, with love, death and danger at their heart.

1900s–Present

Opera is redefined, with more daring use of the voice, including non-verbal sounds such as shrieks and clicks. Plots increasingly deal with up-to-date events.

CHORAL

A choir is a group of people who sing together, and choral music is work for a collection of voices. Choirs come in many sizes, from small chamber choirs to large symphonic choirs.

Depending on the size of the choir, there may be different sections. Each section is responsible for singing specific vocal parts:

Soprano – a high female voice.

Alto – a low female voice.

Contralto – the lowest female voice.

Tenor – a high male voice.

Baritone – a male's voice that is in the middle range, in between tenor and bass.

Bass – a low male voice.

Treble – Usually a young male's voice, sometimes called a boy soprano, who can reach high notes before their voice breaks. You'll hear these in cathedral choirs.

A **conductor** leads the choir, guiding the singers in terms of timing, dynamics and interpretation of the music.

🎵 Laura Mvula's 'Sing to the Moon'

Laura Mvula (1986–present) is best-known as a soul and pop singer-songwriter, but Mvula is classically trained. She studied at the Royal Birmingham Conservatoire. In 2018, 'Sing to the Moon' was performed at the celebrated classical music festival the BBC Proms. It drew on gospel music and spirituals (African-American hymns), as well as English church music.

1600s
Motets (short pieces for choir based on religious texts) can be heard in churches.

1500s
The era of madrigals (short unaccompanied songs for voices alone). The voices weave in and out of one another in a complex polyphonic web of sound.

1700s
A growth in popularity of oratorios and cantatas (pieces for soloists, choir and orchestra that tell stories).

♪ Eric Whitacre's *Lux Aurumque*

Eric Whitacre (1970–present) is celebrated for his use of tech with choirs. He has used the internet to bring his own music to a wider audience, encouraging people to upload recordings of themselves singing his work. One of his pieces, *Lux Aurumque*, included 185 singers from 12 countries.

♪ Georg Friedrich Händel's 'Hallelujah Chorus' from *Messiah*

Georg Friedrich Händel (1685–1759) wrote oratorios (large pieces for soloists, choir and orchestra that tell religious stories) and anthems (grand pieces for choir that celebrated a state occasion or major event).

1800s

Choirs become larger... there are choral festivals that feature thousands of singers performing simultaneously!

1900s-Present

There are no set forms or rules. Composers like John Tavener write reflective music inspired by their religious faith, while Ernst Toch asks a choir to chant the names of countries from around the world in his *Geographical Fugue*.

CHAMBER

Chamber music is intimate music-making for one or a handful of instruments, designed for performance in homes, at parties or in small venues. The ensemble (group of players) was designed to be able to fit into a small room, or 'chamber'.

In the 1800s, industrialisation and developments in technology meant that instruments were becoming more affordable. The piano became the centre of many middle-class homes, with families gathering around it to sing or play duets. It was often seen as a form of relaxation.

There are many different combinations of instruments in chamber music, including:

String Quartet – two violins, a viola and a cello.

Piano Trio – a piano, violin and cello.

Piano Duet – one piano, played by two people.

Piano Sonata – a piano played alone.

Wind Quintet – a flute, oboe, clarinet, French horn and bassoon.

In group chamber music, each instrument can step into the spotlight and show off its unique colours, while enjoying a dialogue with the instruments around it: the ultimate musical conversation!

♫ Joseph Haydn's 'The Lark String Quartet', 1st movement

Joseph Haydn (1732–1809) was the first major composer to create music that was designed for a string quartet. Here, he uses the instruments to imitate the sounds of birdsong.

1600s
Suites (individual musical pieces or movements, with a common theme, performed together) for dancing and trio sonatas (three instruments) become very popular.

1500s
Toccatas and preludes act as introductions to larger pieces, concerts or church services.

1700s
The sonata develops: a piece that spotlights a single instrument.

Johannes Brahms' Horn Trio, 4th movement 🎵

Johannes Brahms' (1833–1897) Horn Trio premiered in Switzerland in 1865. One critic was so shocked by its unusual combination of horn, violin and piano that they refused to accept it was a piece of music at all!

HMPH! *This isn't music at all!*

Nkeiru Okoye's 'Dusk' from *African Sketches* 🎵

Nkeiru Okoye (1972–present) composed *African Sketches*, a collection of piano pieces, inspired by childhood years in Nigeria, with four movements: 'The Village Children at Play', 'Dusk', 'Dancing Barefoot in the Rain' and 'Drums Calling'.

1800s

First performed at home, chamber music moves to the concert hall. It becomes as complex, large-scale and dramatic as many symphonies.

1900s–Present

Experimentation with instruments is the order of the day! Among them is the bonkers *Helicopter String Quartet* by Karlheinz Stockhausen, which places four string players in four helicopters!

27

SCREEN MUSIC

If you've been to a cinema or played a video game, you've heard classical music. Many blockbuster movies, like *Star Wars*, employ a full symphony orchestra to record the score (the full soundtrack).

Music helps heighten the emotion of a scene, speeds it up or slows it down. Underscore is music that plays while characters speak, providing a deeper understanding of a character's emotions. Then there are leitmotifs: short musical ideas linked with specific characters. Film composer Max Steiner once said "music should be felt and not heard."

Then there are video games. Many games offer over 100 hours of narrative, and this all requires musical accompaniment. Everyone from Paul McCartney to Just Blaze has contributed to them.

Theatre, cinema, concert hall or living room... classical music is everywhere!

♫ Koji Kondo's 'Gusty Garden Galaxy' from *Super Mario Galaxy*

Koji Kondo (1961–present) has written many of the classic video game scores for Nintendo, from *Super Mario* to *The Legend of Zelda*. His musical life began at the electric organ, which he learned from the age of five. Kondo started composing for video games after spotting an advert at his school for a new job with Nintendo.

1927
The Jazz Singer is released, the first feature-length film to have recorded and synchronised music and speech, the first of the so-called 'talkies'.

1890s
Films are silent. Any music during a screening is played live by a pianist or organist sitting inside the cinema.

1930s
A golden age for the all-singing, all-dancing movie musicals, where songs help tell the story.

John Williams' 'Superman Theme' 🎵

John Williams (1932–present) began his career as a jazz pianist before scoring films like *Star Wars*, *Jaws* and *Harry Potter*. In his 1978 theme to *Superman*, a brass fanfare shows our hero has arrived, the main trumpet melody leaping upwards as he flies through the air. The instruments almost become characters themselves.

1970s
Composer Wendy Carlos starts using the Moog synthesiser (an instrument that makes sound electronically) to create eerie and atmospheric music in films.

1978
Tomohiro Nishikado's *Space Invaders* is the first video game to have a continuous soundtrack. Composing video game music becomes very popular, using new systems and technology.

2000s–Present
As recording technology becomes more widely available, a single composer regularly crosses between film, video game and concert hall work.

1098–1179
Hildegard of Bingen

Here's someone who was, in every sense, a visionary. Hildegard of Bingen had visions of God and wrote them down as poems and music.

Music was just one part of a lifetime of interests. Hildegard of Bingen – named after the German town she came from – was (deep breath) a nun, diplomat, writer, leader, adviser, plant expert, scientist, public speaker... and a composer. But it all came back to faith. Hildegard became a nun aged 15 and later created her own monastery with 18 sisters. As if that wasn't enough, Hildegard then developed her own language and alphabet, possibly to help bring her nuns together. She used her talents – for music and for words – to unite people. It was all ultimately about expression. Hildegard wrote books on natural history, plants and medicine, and was even the first person to write a morality play, a drama where good battles evil (think *Star Wars*, but in the 1100s). That made her the 'influencer' of the time!

She became a pen pal of popes, kings, emperors and archbishops, and was herself a major public leader: she went on at least four public speaking tours of Germany. This was bold stuff, given that women of the time were not allowed to travel as preacher-teachers; she was in many ways an early feminist, championing the rights of women and dealing with men on an equal footing. No wonder why, in the centuries after her death, Hildegard was considered for sainthood by no less than four different popes!

♫ LISTEN!

A Feather on the Breath of God sung by Gothic Voices

Hildegard was a little-known name even in musical circles, until early music became widely performed and recorded from the 1970s onwards. One of the standouts is this album, released in 1985.

Hildegard's Sound

Her music is often monophonic – a single line, a tune on its own (*mono* means one, *phonic* means sound). This creates a sense of calm, perfect for a focused, intense contemplation of faith. Hildegard wrote mostly sacred plainchant (where people all sing the same line, with religious texts used for the words), intended for use in church: her abbey consisted of 50 nuns who all had trained voices and would sing daily. It's believed a Benedictine nun at the time would sing for eight hours each day! With an in-house choir, then, an abbey provided an ideal testing ground for new music. Music becomes a form of prayer, and having everyone sing the same line creates a powerful symbol of togetherness through faith.

Learning by Ear

The Greeks were the first to use letters of the alphabet to represent different notes. Yet until the Middle Ages, almost all music was passed down the generations by mouth, instead of being written down. There was a lot to learn: in the 600s, monks in churches are estimated to have memorised 80 hours of music, all by ear! By the 900s, it took around 10 years to teach a young chorister all the pieces they'd need to know for future services. And you think school is intense...

Claudio Monteverdi

1567-1643

This composer helped establish opera as a serious storytelling form, writing the first operatic masterpiece, *Orfeo*, in 1607.

Claudio Monteverdi started professional life in his early 20s, working as a violinist in the court of a noble family in Mantua, Italy. Here, he met some of the best and brightest in the arts, including top poets. These writers would soon be providing the words that Monteverdi would set to music.

Opera began as an entertainment for royal families and wealthy noblemen, but it gradually became something for the public to enjoy too. Venice opened its first-ever public opera house in 1637 and this led Monteverdi to write some of his great stage works (all in old age). His crowning achievement, the opera *L'incoronazione di Poppea* ('The Coronation of Poppea') was written when he was 76 years old. Exploring the life of ancient Roman Emperor Nero, this was the first opera to take its plot from real-life history, rather than exploring a myth or fictional tale. Presenting characters based on real people, Monteverdi liked that he could show a raw emotion that made them a human rather than a cardboard caricature. Monteverdi said that the aim of all good music is to 'stir our souls'. He did this by placing greater emphasis on the words; he saw how music could highlight their meaning: a sound equivalent of underlining or highlighting a sentence. This made the meaning of his works clear and his pieces powerfully emotional, leading some audiences of the time to break down in tears. Perhaps he was able to tap into the raw emotions of his characters because he had suffered too. Monteverdi lost his mother when he was a child, and later his wife too, and he channelled his grief into his work.

That Monteverdi chap is a musical marvel!

It would appear so, my lord!

🎵 LISTEN!

'Pur Ti Miro' (I Adore You) from the opera *L'incoronazione di Poppea*

This duet is a love song from the 1600s. Listen to how the two voices weave in and out of each other, sometimes clashing and sometimes fitting together, to suggest the pleasure and pain of love.

Monteverdi's Sound

Expect bolder dissonance with Monteverdi's music: notes can clash strongly and take longer to be resolved, building the tension and that sense of heightened emotion. The most dramatic high-points of a story become a dramatic high-point for the music: the sounds mirror what you see on stage. It's not music for its own sake, but to help tell the story. Monteverdi's sound changed over time, as opera became more mainstream. His later operas are awash with gorgeous tunes and a wider range of characters, because now opera had to be broader, more direct and more exciting in order to make money.

Orfeo

Monteverdi's first opera represents the first truly successful coming-together of words, music, costumes and scenery to tell a story: the earliest enduring and recognisable example of opera. In this epic love story, Orfeo loses the love of his life, Euridice, to a snake bite, and decides to venture into Hell to retrieve her. A totally normal and down-to-earth plot, then, with typically understated emotions (not). Intense feelings, bold gestures and dramatic scenarios would become opera's trademark, largely as a result of Monteverdi.

BARBARA STROZZI

Long before Ed Sheeran and Taylor Swift, there was THIS trailblazing singer-songwriter.

In 1600s Italy, Barbara Strozzi became famous as a singer who wrote music to showcase her own voice. Touchingly, her poet father, Giulio Strozzi, would pen the words that she then set to music. The first such volume was published when Strozzi was just 25. Far from palace courts or public concert venues, she'd perform these songs in the family home in Venice, which became a meeting place for the city's bright and brainy. Despite Strozzi's music-making being remarkably home-based, her name became well known and her music well published: more than 100 of her works were printed and released in her lifetime. This was not always the case for women at this time; she was often the only woman in the room. Add to that the fact she became a single mum to three children, and you get a sense of the challenges she faced.

But Strozzi had all the credentials. Her father had worked with Claudio Monteverdi as a librettist, writing the words for his operas, and her own music teacher had been a pupil of the opera master. Yet Strozzi did not write an opera or sing in one. She focused on a specific genre of writing, mostly composing non-religious songs for soprano voices. A teenager sitting at home, strumming a guitar and writing songs about their latest breakup. That might sound like your sibling, or you, but Strozzi did it first, accompanying herself on the lute (a stringed instrument, much like today's guitar), as she sang original songs.

A woman... writing music?!

I'm not sure that's a good idea...

SHHH!

Goodness! Such a wonderful sound!

♫ LISTEN!

'Che Si Può Fare' ('What Can Be Done')

Listen to the bass line of this piece from 1664 and you'll hear something that sounds quite modern. It's a repeating pattern, like the loops and repeated chord progressions in pop songs, that's designed to stick in your mind.

Strozzi's Sound

Strozzi's songs regularly explore the theme of love and are often strikingly dramatic, using the music to paint the meaning of the words. The word 'death', for example, might be heard just as the music hits a crashing discord, an ugly sound. Using something called *stile concitato* ('agitated style') Strozzi rapidly repeats notes or flutters between two notes, conveying the angst or rage of the words being sung. The speed of a piece might suddenly change, or a word might be repeated several times. Strozzi's music is perfectly designed for a singer to perform and express themselves.

A Man's World?

The role of women in music-making was, for centuries, largely domestic and mostly confined to performance. If a woman wrote music, then small keyboard pieces or little songs were the most that was expected, and it was rare for such works to be anything other than a single handwritten paper copy. To have your work reprinted and distributed across the continent, as Strozzi did, was a noteworthy achievement. As was having her name printed on the sheet music. Well into the 1800s, women writers often used a male pseudonym (a false name) pretending to be a man, so they could have their music heard. Strozzi wrote under her own name, becoming one of the first women composers to be recognised in their own lifetime.

JOHANN SEBASTIAN
BACH
1685-1750

Imagine if your schoolteacher was one of the world's greatest-ever composers!

German composer Johann Sebastian Bach was regarded highly by some of the biggest names in history. Scientist genius Albert Einstein once said: "Give me Bach, Bach, and more Bach" and Ludwig van Beethoven described him as "the immortal God of harmony."

During his life, Bach was famed as a keyboard and organ player, known for his improvising. Impressively, Bach was largely self-taught. Through his teens, he would spend hours copying out by hand the works of other composers to absorb their style. Aged 20, he supposedly walked over 480 kilometres in 10 days to hear a top organist. Bach took learning seriously, so it's appropriate that he went on to become a top teacher. In his late 30s, he was appointed cantor (choir leader in a church setting) at the school of St Thomas in Leipzig,

Germany, where he led choirs and music lessons across four churches. This job required Bach to pen new pieces for services every week, making him a prolific composer.

Bach was a devout Christian and much of his music was religious, including huge-scale works for solo voices, choir and orchestra, known as the Passions, that tell the Bible's Easter Story. Yet he was also happy writing about everyday things. His *Coffee Cantata* is all about coffee!

During his life and for decades after his death, Bach's own music was seen as over-complicated at a time when music was becoming leaner and cleaner. Only in the 1800s did he gain wider recognition. Today, his pieces are the bedrock of training for most pianists and organists. In a way, he continues to teach us all.

♫ LISTEN!

Toccata and Fugue in D minor

This is a showpiece, with fast notes spanning the full range of high and low. It's designed to impress the audience, showing off the instrument and its player.

Bach's Sound

Bach's music is often thick with notes. It's said he once played the keyboard with the help of a stick held in his mouth, since every finger was already in use! Despite the density to his sound, every dot is placed precisely on the music sheet, with frequent patterns and sequences. The figures and shapes you hear in the opening seconds often form the basis of the entire piece that follows. Each piece is a sound mountain built on logic.

Bach as Teacher

Many of Bach's pieces were written to help stretch his students and his own children (he had 20!). When his eldest son, Wilhelm Friedemann, celebrated his ninth birthday, Bach gave him a set of new pieces as a gift, the *Two-Part Inventions* and *Sinfonias*. These are now standard works on record and in concert halls, yet they started as a casual birthday present! Teaching in the classroom, Bach didn't always get on with his pupils. He was accused of fighting a student after calling them a "nanny-goat bassoonist" (whatever that is). Bach drew his sword on the pupil after the boy hit him with a stick, and the pair had to be forced apart by other students.

JOSEPH BOLOGNE
CHEVALIER DE SAINT-GEORGES   1745-1799

This composer has been nicknamed 'the Black Mozart', but it's time he was celebrated for his own name.

For years, Joseph Bologne was known to the French public as a fencer. He enlisted at a fencing academy aged 13 and by the age of 17 was so good that he became a knight, hence the name 'Chevalier'.

Bologne was born on a plantation on the Caribbean islands of Guadeloupe. His father was a French plantation owner and his mother an enslaved woman of African heritage. Bologne moved to Paris when he was 13, and little is known of his musical beginnings. In the 1770s, Bologne's profile was raised when he led an orchestra, soon to be celebrated as the best in France, in a series of public concerts called the Concert Spirituel. No wonder he was then invited to play music with Queen Marie Antoinette of France.

Despite his successes, Bologne encountered a great deal of racism. He would challenge those who threw racist insults to a duel in the fencing ring. He is said to have lost only once in his lifetime.

Given his celebrity status, victory in such fights was seen as a high-profile win in the struggle against slavery in the 1700s. Often the only Black man in the room, Bologne's successful musical career sent a powerful message. He was also a gifted swimmer, dancer and even a fashion icon, with his colourful outfits setting the trend in fashionable Paris.

When the French Revolution took place in 1789, all French citizens were established as equal. Bologne welcomed the changes and offered his services to the Army, joining the first all-Black regiment in Europe and rising to the rank of colonel. He was deployed to the Caribbean to fight against slavery, yet still managed to be involved with concerts when he had a minute! So, forget 'Black Mozart'; Bologne was a star in his own right.

🎵 LISTEN!

Violin Concerto no. 10 in G major: Presto

Presto means 'fast', and lots of fast notes here would certainly have given Bologne the chance to showcase his own dazzling violin-playing.

Bologne's Sound

With two symphonies and six operas to his name, Bologne's music often exudes confidence and bravado, a mirror to the powerhouse man behind it. Perhaps we can also hear his non-musical activities shaping his musical ones. In his concerti, ideas shoot from soloist to orchestra and back again, much like a swordfight. You can also hear Bologne, the violinist: his pieces are full of runs – fast passages that shoot up and down, high and low – designed to show off his playing skills.

It is an honour to play for you, Your Majesty!

Chineke!

'Championing change and celebrating diversity in classical music' – that's the motto of the Chineke! Foundation, created in 2015. At the organisation's heart is the Chineke! Orchestra, Europe's first majority-Black and ethnically diverse orchestra. They've programmed music by Bologne, as well as Chiquinha Gonzaga, the first woman conductor in Brazil, and Fela Sowande, celebrated as the father of modern Nigerian classical music.

Wolfgang Amadeus Mozart

1756–1791

Mozart is arguably one of history's most famous children. He was a touring celebrity by the age of six and died at 35. In that short life, he managed to define the Classical era with his music.

The Mozart family lived in Salzburg, Austria. When Leopold Mozart came home to find his four-year-old son sitting with pen and paper, and asked what he was doing, his son's answer was: "I'm writing a concerto for the piano". So Leopold began taking the young Mozart and his sister Nannerl on tours around Europe.

In London, Mozart played the keyboard with composer-pianist Johann Christian Bach (one of Johann Sebastian Bach's 20 children!). Mozart would sit on Bach's knee and together they would play a piece. The trick was to make the audience believe only one person was playing. Mozart's other stunt was to play blindfolded!

Mozart also wrote a lot of music – and fast. In 1786, he took a single month to pen his opera *The Marriage of Figaro* – one of the most performed operas today, and revolutionary for its time, telling the story of servants who end up teaching their masters. In 1788, he completed his celebrated Symphony no. 40 in just ten days, while writing three piano concerti at the same time. This remarkably passionate piece would be the penultimate (next to last) symphony Mozart would write.

Many of Mozart's works were written amid the hubbub of everyday life, which is probably why he was appreciated by people from all backgrounds. Hairdressers commented how he was a nightmare because when an idea struck, he'd jump out of the chair to work on it.

My boy, you are a genius!

I'm writing a concerto, Father!

Mozart's Sound

Mozart was unusual in that he was a master of every area of writing, from symphonies to concerti to operas to string quartets. He allowed these genres to lend each other a part of their own sound. His piano sonatas sing like songs, while his symphonies can sound like dramas, where every instrument is a character.

The Mozart Conspiracy

Ever since Mozart died, rumours circulated that he had been poisoned by a jealous rival, composer Antonio Salieri. The pair often competed against each other to win commissions (the opportunity to be paid to write a piece for a specific occasion). However, the Salieri poisoning was proven to be untrue. Salieri even went on to teach Mozart's youngest son. It's believed Mozart died of an illness.

♫ LISTEN!

Eine kleine Nachtmusik ('A Little Night Music')

This serenade for string orchestra is the pop song of the 1700s. In the opening Allegro, the strings play the same loud, attention-grabbing statement together. It tells the audience to be quiet and listen!

41

MARIA THERESIA
VON PARADIS

1759–1824

International keyboard player, singer, organist and concerto composer, meet one of the eighteenth century's most multitalented music stars.

Maria von Paradis was born in Vienna, Austria, in 1759. Her father was the imperial secretary in the court of Empress Maria Theresa, who casually became her godmother, and is who she was named after. A sign that von Paradis was destined to become musical royalty!

With the supervision of her royal godmother, von Paradis received the best education possible, even studying with the famous rival of Mozart, Antonio Salieri (a royal favourite). She soon became an in-demand pianist and organist, touring her music in London and Paris. One of von Paradis's greatest gifts was an incredible memory – she memorised more than 60 concerti!

But von Paradis encountered obstacles to her success; she became blind at the age of three. Her friend, the librettist Johann Riedinger, created a wooden pegboard device to help her compose. Variously sized and shaped pegs each represented different note pitches and lengths.

🎵 LISTEN!

'Sicilienne' in E-flat major

A *sicilienne* is a slow and gentle dance, traditionally linked with the countryside; it conjures up images of sunshine and rolling hills. This was performed by the then 19-year-old cellist Sheku Kanneh-Mason at the Royal Wedding in 2018.

With the help of this pegboard, von Paradis wrote five operas, two piano concerti and sixteen piano sonatas. Although she didn't write a huge amount of music – about 30 pieces in all – the works themselves were often on a large scale. Mozart wrote a concerto for her to play, too.

It wasn't all about her, either. In 1808, von Paradis created and headed up her own music school in Vienna, designed expressly for talented young female musicians. She taught there too, leading piano and voice classes for more than a decade, right up to the year she died.

Nicknamed 'the blind enchantress', von Paradis was a phenomenon in her age. While Mozart was buried in a pauper's grave, von Paradis was laid to rest in a grand mausoleum. She overcame disability and proved what she was capable of. Although she couldn't see, she could hear and feel, demonstrating that music is in us all.

Von Paradis's Sound

Von Paradis wrote in the style of her contemporaries Mozart and Joseph Haydn. The emphasis is on balance and symmetry, poise and elegance, with transparent textures and singing melodies.

I wrote this concerto for you, Maria!

Blind Musicians

Celebrated musicians who have been sight-impaired or blind include Spain's Joaquín Rodrigo, who wrote one of the most popular concerti of all time, the *Concierto de Aranjuez*, written for guitar and orchestra. He was blind from the age of three and never even played the guitar!

Japanese concert pianist Nobuyuki Tsujii began playing on toy pianos by ear aged two, and has gone on to perform at Britain's BBC Proms and at New York's world-renowned Carnegie Hall.

Other famous sight-impaired musicians include the legendary Stevie Wonder and jazz singer Diane Schuur, who both pioneered music in their genres.

LUDWIG VAN
BEETHOVEN
1770–1827

Many of Beethoven's greatest works were written when he could hardly hear at all, yet he changed the landscape of classical music forever.

From the age of 26, Ludwig van Beethoven began losing his hearing. His friends noticed how out of tune his piano had become, but Beethoven couldn't tell. When he reached his 40s, his friends had to write down their conversations with the composer, as he couldn't hear their replies at all. But it was during this time that he composed some of his most noteworthy pieces.

Beethoven's early life was not easy and music was an escape. Born in Bonn, Germany, in December 1770, he left school early, at the age of 11. It's thought he may have suffered from dyslexia. He became a father-like figure for his brothers after their dad, who was an alcoholic, lost his job. At one point he considered suicide, and he himself said that the one thing saving him was music. He went on to compose groundbreaking symphonies, concerti, sonatas and quartets.

Beethoven was an outsider. People often thought he was mad. He once broke a chair over a prince in a fit of rage and was known to throw eggs at waiters if he didn't like the food they'd served. His eccentricities led many to doubt his value as a musician. Fellow composer Carl Maria von Weber described Beethoven's later music as 'confused chaos'.

But Beethoven forced music to grow up. It became more outwardly emotional, harmonically daring, epically long or shamelessly short. With Beethoven, music stopped being polite or in any way predictable. Beethoven pointed to the future, paving the way for the Romantic era of the 1800s. He remains one of music's great visionaries.

♫ LISTEN!

'Eroica' Symphony, 1st movement

This was originally dedicated to the French leader Napoleon, who, at the time, was a symbol of freedom. The piece shocked contemporary audiences for its great length and seriousness.

Beethoven's Sound

Beethoven's music was longer, harder, larger and louder than anything that had been heard before. Where symphonies might have lasted 20 minutes, Beethoven was writing hour-long stretches. Where past works were divided into three or four movements, Beethoven wrote five in his Sixth Symphony. Beethoven created a richer sound as the orchestra expanded to 50 or 60 players, and the violins were no longer the only instruments to carry the main tune.

BAH!

*Other people's music is **SO** predictable!*

Caution!
Composer at Work

Back in the 1800s, you might have spotted Beethoven on a walk, singing (badly) at the top of his voice and shaking his arms wildly. He would develop hundreds of sketches for a single piece, reworking and revising the original idea. Walking and singing proved the ideal way of working out the music in his mind. He'd then rush back home and scribble down the notes he'd imagined. Beethoven also wrote in the bathroom. He would get very hot while composing, so he'd plunge his head into cold water to keep cool – and to keep himself awake. If neighbours found water dripping from their ceilings, that meant Beethoven was at work.

Richard Wagner

1813-1883

Wagner had a lot to say and did things his way. He pushed music to its limits and revolutionised storytelling – but he is also a controversial figure.

Richard Wagner wrote the libretto (text) and the music for his operas, making him composer, poet, producer, philosopher and more. His ultimate aim was to create a 'total work of art', where every aspect of an opera helped tell the story. He created epic dramas with huge orchestras, a lush sound and powerful singers.

Born in Leipzig, Germany, Wagner is believed to be the son of an actor, who put him on the stage while he was still a child. Wagner's early aims were to become a playwright. By the age of 20, he had written his first opera.

Over time, Wagner's music almost became a religion, with devoted disciples (and equally vocal critics). Key to this Wagner cult was his very own festival, for which he built his own theatre in the German town of Bayreuth, particularly to showcase his epic masterpiece the Ring Cycle, a collection of four operas performed over four nights. It takes around 15 hours to perform in full, but that's nothing compared to the 26 years Wagner took to write it!

Perhaps unsurprisingly for someone with such ambition, Wagner had a huge ego. At parties, he screamed at the top of his voice if he felt he wasn't getting enough attention. He gambled violently, and once even staked his mum's pension (thankfully he won the bet, so didn't have to give all her money away). Wagner did things his way, pushing music to its limits, challenging tradition and redefining what drama could be.

> Put it all on **BLACK** and let it ride!

♫ LISTEN!

Prelude to *Tristan und Isolde*

Wagner wrote this sensuous opera – a love story – while he himself was falling in love. He translates his yearning heart into music of great longing and emotional tension, full of clashes without resolution, questions without answers.

To Listen or Not to Listen...

Can we separate a person from their music? Can we enjoy music written by someone who had political and social views so against everything we believe in today? Wagner is the prime subject of such questions. In 1850, he published a pamphlet that was openly antisemitic (racist towards Jews). Later, 1930s Nazi Germany took antisemitism to horrifying extremes in the Holocaust, and Wagner was one of the favourite composers of Nazi leader Adolf Hitler. Wagner's operas speak of German mythical heroes, struggles and nationhood; little wonder they appealed to the Nazis. Should this mean we avoid his music?

Wagner's Sound

His music is often heavy and rich, perhaps to match his surroundings: he liked to work in a room pumped full of thick perfume. His operas try to do the same; the music is indulgent, sensuous and sometimes almost overpowering. Wagner was also one of the main developers of the leitmotif (where a character has their own theme).

47

Giuseppe Verdi

1813–1901

Police were stopping traffic. The hotel was closed to other guests. The king got updates every hour. Verdi, Italy's hero, was dying. His loss was a national tragedy – quite a rise from his humble origins.

Giuseppe Verdi (Joseph Green, to you and me) was born in the north of Italy to a couple who ran a local pub; in his words, he was 'totally ignorant' about music and everything else. He taught himself how to play the piano. When he applied for music school in Milan, he was turned down because he played the piano badly and was considered too old to learn. Aged 18, Verdi had been written off. He'd show them! He went on to become a hard-working composer, sometimes writing for 15 hours each day. He could work from 5 a.m. to 6 p.m. without a break, eating nothing and only drinking coffee. Unsurprisingly, Verdi often suffered bad health after writing an opera, having to visit a spa to get some rest. Music was draining!

The composer lived to see the day Italy became a single, united country. This was in 1861, and Verdi was even asked to run for the Italian parliament (he served for four years). People asking for an address to which they could send letters were told that all they had to write on the envelope was 'Verdi, Italy'. Everyone knew him. Verdi always said that he came from simple Italian peasant stock, but this wasn't entirely true. He did, however, spend lots of time each year in the rural countryside, planting cabbages and helping with the harvest. Perhaps this helped him make his operas relatable: he understood real people because in many ways he lived a normal life himself. Reflecting a country's worries and playing a part in resolving them, Verdi's example is a tribute to the power of music to bring people together.

Goodness me! He composes like a genius AND harvests like a pro!

♫ LISTEN!

'Va, Pensiero' from the opera *Nabucco*

This chorus rapidly became a hymn to freedom. The words "va, pensiero, sull'ali dorate" ("Go, thought, on wings of gold") became the highlight of Verdi's first major operatic success, *Nabucco*. It expresses the hopes of Jewish people while they are attacked in their homelands.

Verdi's Sound

Verdi was a master of opera. These dramas told through song were the hit musicals of the 1800s. They were produced all around the world, but Italy was their home. Until 1861, Italy was not one country, but a collection of separate states. Verdi's operas hit a sensitive spot with Italian audiences, often exploring themes like freedom, nationhood and oppression. Verdi's music united the Italian people through hummable tunes at a time when the authorities were keeping them divided.

Tight Deadlines

Verdi wrote his music for *Il trovatore* in a single month. Then, while rehearsing that opera on stage, he was writing a whole new one: *La traviata*. Deadlines were tight, and most opera composers of the day were used to churning out between two and four new works every year.

LOUIS MOREAU
GOTTSCHALK
1829-1869

Meet the popular American sensation of the 1800s! A global superstar!

New Orleans-born Louis Moreau Gottschalk played the organ at his local cathedral when he was just seven years old. He went on to become one of the first American musicians to be world-famous. He played the piano (and often his own music) throughout France, Spain, the USA, Cuba, Jamaica, Brazil and Venezuela. It was hard work. In a three-year tour of the USA, Gottschalk gave more than 1,100 concerts (multiple gigs a day) and travelled over 152,000 kilometres. Everything he did seemed to be epic! Later in life, he organised so-called 'monster concerts' with performances including up to 650 players.

Just like pop stars today, Gottschalk was the talk of the town... for more than just his music. His romances were hot gossip. After bad behaviour on one tour, he was chased out of town by a mob of angry locals. On another occasion, a man slammed a carriage door against Gottschalk's hands, jealous of his piano-playing abilities. Then when Gottschalk died at the tender age of 40, it was rumoured a jealous husband had ordered an assassination. Gottschalk is important for representing his era, a time when there were many celebrity pianists who wrote music to showcase their abilities and toured the world as player-composers. Who said pop stars were a modern phenomenon?

♫ LISTEN!

"'La nuit des tropiques' Symphony ('A Night in the Tropics')", 2nd movement

Gottschalk's pieces often suggest certain locations or activities, and this toe-tapper is a dance in the sunshine. African-American percussion instruments sit alongside a full orchestra, creating what is quite possibly the first classical-orchestral version of a samba (an upbeat Brazilian dance). The lively music you might hear on the streets of South America here steps into the concert hall...

Gottschalk's Sound

Gottschalk would often quote other people's music in his own work, an early suggestion of the sampling we now hear in hip hop (where an artist plays a chunk of music or a recording by someone else). His music is all-embracing and often a lot of fun.

NO! Not now! I love this part!

Peculiar Pianists

So you think Gottschalk was eccentric? How about these figures…

Teresa Carreño (1853–1917) Taught by Gottschalk, this Venezuelan became a global star. As a child, she played the piano for US President Abraham Lincoln at the White House (and was bold enough to complain about the quality of the piano). A crater on Venus is now named after her.

Frédéric Chopin (1810–1849) This Polish composer-pianist did not like playing in public. His reputation as a player rests on just 30 concerts!

Ignacy Jan Paderewski (1860–1941) He was not only a concert pianist, but also the prime minister of Poland in 1919. He said it was harder to play the piano than to be a world leader.

Ethel Smyth
1858–1944

Not only did Ethel Smyth fight for herself and for her music,
but she also fought for women's rights, and was arrested in the process!

In the UK, it wasn't until 1928 that women gained the right to vote in elections. Campaigning for this were the suffragettes, and London-born Ethel Smyth was one of their prominent members. She was jailed for two months after throwing a brick through a politician's window. Yet she continued the struggle for equality from her cell... she stuck a toothbrush out of the cell window and conducted the prisoners in the yard outside in a rendition of her own suffragette anthem!

Her childhood home life posed its own challenges. Smyth's father was a military general who objected to her pursuing a career in music, thinking it an unsuitable job for a woman. Young Smyth ended up being taught the piano by a military officer who lived next door... until her father decided to relocate him to a posting on the opposite side of the country, just to stop his daughter having lessons.

Smyth wasn't the sort to give up easily. Soon she refused to go to church and boycotted family dinners. This home-grown campaign lasted a full two years, before her father finally caved in and allowed her to go abroad to study music full-time. The opposition continued in certain circles. One prominent music publisher warned her that no woman composer had ever succeeded, and that some of the women they had published were 'very good' but 'had no sales'. Still, she pushed on.

Before long, Smyth became the most successful British female composer. She was friends with international figures like Johannes Brahms, Clara Schumann and Pyotr Tchaikovsky. She was unusual in gaining international recognition for her operas at a time when women were encouraged to stick to writing small-scale chamber works, if anything at all. Her operas were staged in Berlin and New York.

All together now, ladies!

DEEDS NOT WORDS

♫ LISTEN!

The Wreckers

This opera, completed in 1904, is widely celebrated as Smyth's best work. Full of darkness and violence, the story takes us to a British fishing village. The music is full of colourful writing that suggests the watery setting.

Smyth's Sound

One of her most notable musical contributions was the suffragette song 'The March of the Women', written in 1910 and sung in the streets and at rallies. It became an anthem for gender equality. Smyth's music and her indomitable spirit highlight music's power to bring about social change. Music really can make the world a better place.

WHO ARE THE PEOPLE

Multitalented

Smyth was also a successful writer of words. Ten books flowed from her pen, as well as numerous articles and essays championing women's rights.

53

ARNOLD SCHOENBERG

1874–1951

Here's another musical revolutionary – whose works were so hard to fathom that they made people angry and even caused a riot.

Arnold Schoenberg's beginnings in Vienna, Austria, were far from musical. His parents owned a shoe shop. Young Schoenberg taught himself about music from an encyclopedia. When his father died, the 15-year-old worked in a bank to earn money for the family. He was so poor, he had to walk to concerts (often more than 16 kilometres each way) as he couldn't afford train tickets.

His is a career of tenacity and hard work. Later, when Schoenberg was told his Violin Concerto was so difficult it needed a player with six fingers, he replied: "Very well, I can wait." His music is not singable and is difficult to understand on first hearing. But whether you like it or not, you have to admire Schoenberg's insistence on trying something new. He made people question exactly what 'music' can mean…

Schoenberg had a circle of followers, almost like disciples. He and two key students, Anton Webern and Alban Berg, became known as the Second Viennese School (a school of thought, not a literal school; the 'First' being Joseph Haydn, Mozart and Beethoven). They had a difficult time getting their music to be appreciated. At one of their concerts in 1913, the audience burst out laughing. This soon became an actual riot. Angry concertgoers fought on the stage and the police arrived. It took half an hour for the madness to die down, and the evening resulted in a court case. One doctor testified that such music was dangerous to the nervous system. Schoenberg's music proved violent, in more ways than one. In fact, a newspaper in Vienna reported one of his concerts in its crime section, rather than in the arts pages!

♫ LISTEN!

Pierrot lunaire

The character who sings this song cycle (a group of songs that tell a story) is a nightmarish clown, 'Moonstruck Pierrot'. The singer uses something called 'speech-song' (Schoenberg's student Alban Berg called it *Sprechstimme*), which is halfway between singing and talking. The effect can be terrifying. The piece was written in 1912, before Schoenberg devised the 12-note technique – so it's atonal rather than serial (see page 55).

Schoenberg's Sound

Schoenberg introduced a new system of composing, based on the ordering of notes. Under his 12-note technique (also known as serialism), the composer can't repeat the same note until each of the remaining 11 has been sounded in a fixed order. Through this method, every note is equal. It leads to lines of music that jump wildly from one note to the next. Under Schoenberg, logic, system and structure become key governing ideas over a piece. At one concert of music by Schoenberg's protégé Anton Webern, a musician actually stormed off stage shouting, "This is maths, not music!" British composer Ernest J. Moeran described Schoenberg's compositions as 'wrong note music'.

Tonality versus Atonality

Tonal music is music based on a specific key (a number of flats and sharps – the black notes on a piano). Tonality is a bit like gravity, or different rooms in the same house: everything is kept in check around a given point. In atonal music, keys are absent. It's an open field rather than a straight corridor. This means that a piece often jumps from high notes to low notes but without returning to a clear centre or anchor. This way of writing became popular among many twentieth-century composers.

IGOR STRAVINSKY

1882-1971

Stravinsky was once described as a 'cave man of music'. Ouch! And it turns out that riots are surprisingly common in classical music.

Russian composer Igor Stravinsky was, at the age of 30, shaking up the classical world with a series of pieces written for ballet. His third one for a dance company called the Ballets Russes was called *The Rite of Spring*. It was full of violent, dissonant music and angry, driving rhythms. The story follows the sacrifice of a young girl. Grace and elegance were replaced by violence and raw power.

It should really have been called 'The Riot of Spring', as the audience on the first night (in May 1913), shocked by its sound, broke out into fighting. The choreographer (the person who designed the dance routine) was forced to stand on a chair and beat a regular pulse to try to keep the dancers moving in time with the music, because the orchestra was struggling to be heard. The lights were flicked on and off to try to stop the brawl, and the police came to break it up.

But Stravinsky was far from being a 'bad boy' of music. He was a keen reader, with a library of more than 10,000 books. He put in major hours composing, too; he sometimes wrote for 18 hours each day. All of this might lead us to expect that, as a child, Stravinsky was an amazing student. Far from it. As a boy, he had few friends and found schoolwork fairly challenging. He sat at the piano as a way of fighting loneliness, and preferred improvising to practising set pieces and exercises.

🎵 LISTEN!

The Firebird

Another of Stravinsky's ballets, it's inspired by a Russian folk story about a bird whose magical feathers help rescue a princess held captive under the spell of an evil sorcerer. Listen to the stirring finale: a solo horn sings a noble melody over shimmering strings and harp, and gradually other instruments join in. It's one big crescendo (it gets louder and fuller) that ends in a blazing fanfare: the triumph of the beautiful firebird rising into the skies.

Stravinsky's Sound

Stravinsky went from childhood loneliness to becoming one of the key composers of the 1900s, exploring a range of styles. Following the violence of *The Rite of Spring*, he began to write music that was closer in style to that of earlier centuries, using smaller orchestras that looked back to the lightness and tunefulness of music in Mozart's day. This was a trend called neoclassicism. Then, in later years, Stravinsky wrote experimental atonal works (where a piece has no key, no anchor or centre of gravity, which often results in harsh, angular and dissonant music). His musical language changed throughout his life.

Is This a Theatre or a Zoo?

Perhaps one of the strangest requests that came Stravinsky's way was for a ballet for elephants. A circus approached a choreographer with the idea and, in 1942, Stravinsky wrote his jolly *Circus Polka* to accompany 50 elephants and 50 showgirls at New York's Madison Square Garden.

57

FLORENCE PRICE
1887–1953

In 2009, in Illinois, USA, an old, abandoned house was found to be an unlikely treasure chest of African-American classical music history.

This building had been the home of composer Florence Price for more than 50 years. The attic contained stacks of old papers and music sheets, including two unpublished violin concerti.

Price was born in Little Rock, Arkansas, in 1887. Her mother was a music teacher, so it's little surprise that Price was playing the piano by the age of four. She moved north to Chicago in 1927, trying to escape the racial violence and oppression of America's southern states. In Chicago, greater freedom and opportunity allowed her creativity to blossom. Price played the organ in cinemas for silent films and composed songs for radio ads.

The year 1932 saw one of her greatest triumphs. Her Symphony in E minor won a major composition award and highlighted the importance of African-American music in the classical sphere.

The symphony was inspired by a **spiritual** (an African-American hymn that often draws on the experience of slavery). When the Chicago Symphony Orchestra performed it the following year, Price became the first African-American woman to have her music played by a major orchestra.

Never in Vain

Although Price's music was often performed in her lifetime, little of it was published. This meant it only survived after her death because of the handwritten scores she left behind, scores that for decades lay undiscovered in an attic. But as interest in African-American composers grows and manuscripts are (re)discovered, Florence Price is finally getting the recognition she deserves.

Price's Sound

Price's music brings together the European classical tradition in which she was trained and the haunting melodies of African-American spiritual and folk tunes. She was a deeply religious person, so brought the music of the African-American church into her music, as well as influences from Antonín Dvořák, Pyotr Tchaikovsky and other European Romantic composers. Many of Price's composition titles depict the harsh realities of life that existed for African-Americans who were enslaved just two decades before her birth. Lively rhythms expose sentiments of the difficult days of slavery.

More Treasures

With Price (rightly) celebrated in classical music, there are many more great Black women composers to recognise. Margaret Bonds became the first Black soloist to appear with the Chicago Symphony Orchestra, and composed a major classical work (*Montgomery Variations*) dedicated to civil rights leader Martin Luther King. Undine Smith Moore co-founded the Black Music Center in 1969, becoming 'the Dean of Black Women Composers'.

🎵 LISTEN!

Piano Quintet in A minor, 3rd movement

This quintet was one of the pieces discovered in the house in Illinois and was virtually unknown until then. The third movement is based on the Juba – a West African dance brought to America by enslaved peoples.

59

George Gershwin
1898–1937

He brought jazz into the concert hall and popular song into the opera house. Who needs genres and labels?

Nowhere is this clearer than in *Rhapsody in Blue*, where a classical orchestra plays with more than a *hint* of jazz. It channels the energy of New York City, where George Gershwin lived. He sat writing it in his flat, surrounded by the jangling of cars and trains (some parts were actually written while he travelled in a train carriage), and the clickety-clack of those rhythms slipped into the music. It paints a picture of a composer in New York in his mid-20s. It made Gershwin world-famous.

With hit musicals, concert pieces, film scores and pop songs pouring out of him, Gershwin became one of the biggest musical celebrities of the 1920s. Some say that he was the richest composer of all time, which is quite a rise for someone who as a boy spent most of his time roller skating and playing in the streets.

Nobody in the Gershwin family was a musician – in fact, his father ran a Turkish bathhouse in Harlem. A lot of what Gershwin knew, he had taught himself. He had to buy five books about concerti before writing his own, as he didn't know what a concerto was. When his parents bought a piano, it was for his older brother, Ira. Yet it was George who shocked the family by immediately taking to the keys and playing tunes by ear (without the help of sheet music). Ira ended up becoming George's great collaborator, writing lyrics to his music: it was a sibling partnership.

🎵 LISTEN!

An American in Paris

On a visit to Paris in 1928, Gershwin ended up writing a piece about it. He went around the local markets to purchase French taxi horns for use in the work's first performance in New York. It's a musical postcard!

Gershwin's Sound

Gershwin died at the tragically young age of 38, so his music never stopped having that distinctive youthful exuberance. It's the life and soul of the party, channelling the energy of the USA in the 1920s and the sheer joy of music-making.

No time to talk! Is your piano in tune?

Piano Addiction

Gershwin became a phenomenal pianist, regularly playing for four hours at a time. Fellow composer Harold Arlen (who wrote the melody to the much-loved song 'Over the Rainbow', for the 1939 film *The Wizard of Oz*), recalled how Gershwin would ring the doorbell, rush through to play his piano, and only then say hello! The way he composed was to doodle at the piano, something he sometimes also did in the middle of interviews.

LEONARD BERNSTEIN

1918–1990

**Composer, conductor, lecturer, broadcaster, writer and pianist...
and from classical to Broadway, stage to screen – Bernstein was a master of many trades.**

In 1943, at the age of 25, Leonard Bernstein shot to fame in one of the most celebrated concerts of the last century. He stepped in at short notice to conduct the prestigious New York Philharmonic in a live national broadcast when the main conductor, Bruno Walter, fell ill. Although Bernstein later claimed to have been drunk, the concert was a great success! The next morning, Bernstein was on the front page of the *New York Times*. He later became the first US-born conductor of a major American orchestra, becoming the New York Philharmonic's music director and leading them in more than a thousand concerts.

Bernstein was also a versatile composer. He was at home writing both symphonies and Broadway musicals, including the iconic *West Side Story*, which is a retelling of Shakespeare's *Romeo and Juliet* – a story of lovers from two rival families who will never be able to stay together – reset among the rival gangs of New York.

Bernstein worked hard to promote music among young people. He presented TV shows that explored different areas of classical music, with his orchestra by his side; you can watch these Young People's Concerts on YouTube.

As Bernstein said: "Everyone learns to read words... But almost nobody is taught to read music. It's just another kind of language." Little surprise that as a boy Bernstein would lie in bed reading **sheet music** (the books with all the notes in them) in the way that other children read comics.

On the Ward

Bernstein wrote parts of the 1944 musical *On the Town* in an unlikely place... His writing partner Adolph Green needed to have his tonsils removed, and Bernstein decided it would save time if he had an operation too – meaning they could continue writing the show, in the hospital! So they booked in for the same day and in the same room. Nurses and patients nearby were alarmed by the sounds of laughter and singing that emerged from room 669!

🎵 LISTEN!

'America' (*West Side Story*)

Full of confusing rhythms and sudden gear shifts, this song is sung by a group of characters from Puerto Rico: some explaining their dreams of making it big in America, others singing of the downsides of living there. Stephen Sondheim (who wrote the words) said the idea came to Bernstein when he went on holiday to Puerto Rico and was influenced by Latin America in musical style and instrumentation.

Bernstein's Sound

Music is so much richer for his diverse talents. Although he was frustrated by the lack of time to write, he was a key force in bringing classical music to a wider audience with his TV work; he was a great champion of Gustav Mahler, when this major composer of symphonies was not popular. Also Bernstein was a powerful example of the value of bringing together classical, jazz and popular music. Bernstein really was a master of many trades.

HANS ZIMMER

1957–PRESENT

Bringing a rock and pop sensibility to his film scores, Zimmer has helped bridge the gap between classical music and other genres.

In the 1800s, Beethoven started writing for a larger orchestra, and gave different instruments a starring role. Then in the 1900s, the 'orchestra' came to mean whatever the composer wanted: sirens, propellers and wind machines crop up in the 1920s! So it's not surprising that when electric guitars and drum kits came along, they too took their place in the orchestra… And with regard to this, one man in particular comes to mind.

German composer Hans Zimmer describes himself as a 'musical storyteller'. He's behind the orchestral music for all sorts of films, including *Kung Fu Panda*, *Madagascar*, *The Lion King* and *Pirates of the Caribbean: Dead Man's Chest*. And not only has he introduced different instruments to orchestral writing, but he has also introduced new spaces for concerts. His film music often takes a full orchestra to places like the O2 in London. Zimmer is the rock star of film score writing.

Although he's now helping to redefine classical music, Zimmer at age six hated having piano lessons. He had to play Mozart and lots of exercises, and didn't enjoy reading sheet music (the notes on a page). He never went to music school or university, and describes each film he works on as "a whole new journey of learning". The project is his classroom, the story his teacher. Zimmer has also admitted he suffers from stage fright!

🎵 LISTEN!

'Time' (*Inception*)

This track from the music for the 2010 film *Inception* starts with a solo piano and a gentle background hum of electronics. It's a dramatic piece that unfolds to a shattering climax, before shrinking back to the quiet of the opening. Like a pop song, it repeats a small idea over and over, but Zimmer uses different instruments to give the phrase a varied colour each time.

Genre Explorer

For someone who brings different timbres together, we shouldn't be surprised that Zimmer describes his own listening as being 'all over the place', from 1970s pop supergroup ABBA to 1700s Baroque master Johann Sebastian Bach.

Zimmer's Sound

He's celebrated for bringing together different sounds and instruments, mixing electronics and pop and rock instruments with a huge orchestra. His music often has an epic, dramatic sweep to it.

Nobuo Uematsu

1959- PRESENT

Next time you sit down at a games console, keep an extra ear out for the music – which might well have been written by this Japanese composer.

You might not always be aware of it, but the top orchestras of today are recording symphony-length scores for your gaming pleasure. One of the greatest game storytellers is Nobuo Uematsu. He's mainly associated with Square Enix's *Final Fantasy* franchise, but his music has gone far beyond the screen.

The Latin choral track 'Liberi Fatali' from *Final Fantasy VIII* found its way to the Olympic Games in Athens in 2004, accompanying swimming events there. His game music has also been performed live by full classical orchestras, including at the annual Symphonic Game Music Concerts in Germany, in the UK by the London Symphony Orchestra, and in the US by the celebrated Los Angeles Philharmonic.

It all started with piano lessons at the age of 12. But Uematsu taught himself much of what he knows about music, and claims that the figure who made the greatest impression on him was the pop-rock singer-songwriter Elton John (who, incidentally, studied classical music as a boy).

♫ LISTEN!

'Main Theme' (*Final Fantasy*)

As played by the London Philharmonic Orchestra on the album *The Greatest Video Game Music,* this piece goes from an opening march-like figure into a noble melody for strings. It's rousing stuff to set the scene for a battle against evil.

◄ ● ►

Let's Mosey!

Uematsu has shared that he doesn't get his greatest creative inspiration from listening to music. Instead, he says the best activity to spark a musical idea is walking his dog!

Uematsu's Sound

Uematsu's video game music blurs lines between genres. From electronica to heavy metal to symphonic classical, his style can't be pinned down. He does, however, admit that he always begins composing by writing the melody first. Perhaps that's the key to Uematsu's success. At once hummable and colourful, his work reflects the joy of video games themselves: when no two stories and characters are the same, the music must be similarly all-embracing...

Hmmmm...
Maybe an electric guitar? Or a horn section? **OR BOTH!**

A Motley of Music

What might be on Uematsu's playlist? Alongside Elton John, he's named his influences as the Beatles, the Russian Romantic composer Pyotr Tchaikovsky, rock star Jimi Hendrix, classical innovator Igor Stravinsky, and the percussive sounds of twentieth-century classical composer Carl Orff. (Listen to Orff's 'O Fortuna' from *Carmina Burana* and you'll probably recognise it from TV talent shows... it's what I call 'judge's entrance music'!)

SHIRLEY J. THOMPSON

1958-PRESENT

A rapper, a drum kit, two choirs, solo singers, dhol drummers... and the Royal Philharmonic Orchestra. No wonder she called it 'A 21st Century Symphony'!

Originally a commission (a piece of music requested for a specific event) to mark Queen Elizabeth II's Golden Jubilee in 2002, *New Nation Rising: A 21st Century Symphony* was written as a celebration of London's thousand-year history. The four movements chart the progression of London from rural fields to crowded cityscape. Lilting strings in the opening 'Marshes, Hamlets and Roaming Cows' give way to a toe-tapping rock beat and rap in the final 'New Nation Rising' movement.
It's history, taking us from the past to the present in sound.

Amazingly, British composer Shirley J. Thompson wasn't encouraged towards music as a child. She was told to aim for a career working in factories. But soon she was playing the violin in youth orchestras and went on to study music at university. Thompson has blazed a trail ever since. She is the first woman in Europe to have both composed and conducted a symphony within the last 40 years, and has been named in the *London Evening Standard*'s 'Power List of Britain's Top 100 Most Influential Black People' for seven years in a row. She was also one of 12 composers to write new music for the coronation of King Charles III and Queen Camilla in 2023.

Writing music to mark important historical moments and social change, making classical music representative of diverse cultures and communities, embracing different genres... Thompson represents the melting pot that is classical music, where connections are more important than differences. Who knows where she might take us next...

♫ LISTEN!

'London Symphony Anthem'

This rousing fanfare is a celebration of the city that raised its composer. Its simple melody and words allow anyone to join in, reflecting the uniting spirit of so much of her work.

Music for Children

Thompson has been an influential figure in bringing classical music to a younger audience in the UK. In 2002, she devised the Newham Symphony Schools Spectacular, working with young people aged 7–17; this in turn ballooned into a nationwide music education scheme called Every Child a Musician. In the London Borough of Newham, this scheme provided free music lessons to schools, supporting around 12,500 young people every year.

Ah yes! **THIS** is the one for me!

Thompson's Sound

Thompson's work is celebrated for bringing things together, whether it's different instruments and cultures, or varied media (combining live music with dance, film or spoken word). In 1995, she set up the Shirley Thompson Ensemble in London: a group of instrumental soloists, singers, visual artists and dancers. They combined world, popular and classical music, linked live dance with video projections, and brought together notated music and improvisation.

69

HONOURABLE MENTIONS

When a genre has more than 1,000 years of history and spans the world, there are always more names to discover. Not wanting to miss anyone out, here are some more pointers for your listening: a small selection of important and interesting composers worth exploring...

Guillaume Dufay (c.1400–1474)

Long before hip hop sampling came along, Guillaume Dufay was quoting pre-existing tunes in his music. Born near Brussels, in modern-day Belgium, he was the first composer to frequently use a folk song in his masses: a song whistled by everyday people incorporated into large-scale religious pieces.

Guillaume de Machaut (1300–1377)

French composer Guillaume de Machaut brought emotion and expressiveness into music, saying "he who writes without feeling spoils both his words and music."

Ignatius Sancho (c. 1729–1780)

Ignatius Sancho was born on a slave ship in the middle of the Atlantic Ocean. Although he was enslaved in Britain, he later became a free man and the first Black person to vote in parliamentary elections. Sancho became a composer, and wrote essays in favour of the abolition of the slave trade.

John Dowland (1563–1626)

The lute master of the Renaissance, John Dowland of England, UK, was basically the hit pop singer-songwriter of the 1500s, writing ballads about love and loss.

Antonín Dvořák (1841–1904)

Despite being a citizen of the Austrian Empire, Antonín Dvořák saw himself as Czech, writing operas that used the language and symphonies that channelled their folk songs. Later in life, he ran a music school in New York, and was deeply impressed by hearing African-American spirituals; this helped shape his famous Symphony no.9, *From the New World*.

Will Marion Cook (1869–1944)

A talented violinist, African-American Will Marion Cook played at Carnegie Hall in the US in 1889, only for a critic to call him "the world's greatest Negro violinist." Cook was furious and shouted: "I am not the world's greatest Negro violinist. I am the greatest violinist in the world!" Feeling limited in the classical world by systemic racism, Cook moved into musical theatre and wrote shows for Broadway that featured all-Black casts. He later set up the New York Syncopated Orchestra.

William Grant Still (1895–1978)

A man behind nine operas and five symphonies! In 1931, William Grant Still became the first African-American to have a composition played by a major American orchestra; this was his Symphony no.1, nicknamed the 'Afro-American' for its embrace of the influence of Black American folksong.

Margaret Hubicki (1915–2006)

A pioneering teacher as well as a composer, Margaret Hubicki from England, UK, developed a method of writing down musical notes that helped dyslexic people read music.

INFLUENCE IN MUSIC TODAY

Genres are simply the boxes we pack music into. No composer sits down to write a piece and says "I'll write some classical music today". You write, and the 'genre' is named afterwards. Music is all about freedom – it's the expression of thoughts and feelings – and so it cannot be pinned down. Having said that, many musicians are influenced by different genres, inspiring a 'melting pot' of creativity.

POP STARS WITH CLASSICAL TRAINING

From the age of eleven, pop star Elton John spent five years studying at London's Royal Academy of Music. He enjoyed playing music by Bach and Beethoven, but has said that, even at that age, he knew he didn't want to be a classical pianist. However, he has praised what it taught him, helping to develop his collaboration skills and understanding of how to structure a piece.

Another pop star with classical training is Alicia Keys; she trained as a pianist from the age of seven, and was particularly drawn to melancholic compositions by composers like Frédéric Chopin. She has commented on how her lessons gave her the ability to translate her musical thoughts into something written down.

Lady Gaga is a classically trained pianist. Aged eleven, she was going to join the prestigious Juilliard School of Music in New York, but decided it wasn't for her. However, piano lessons taught her how to play tunes by ear; she preferred this to reading sheet music, where you read and play from notes on a page.

Minimalism

This movement began in the 1960s, as a reaction against the very mathematical, complex and dense scores coming from experimental European writers. One of the first major minimalist works is *In C*, written in 1964 by Terry Riley; it is made of 53 short, numbered musical ideas which musicians can choose at random, playing them in any order and repeating them for as long as they like. This way, it's a musical mosaic pieced together by the players themselves.

From the Sitar to the Guitar, India to Indiana

Indian sitar player and composer Ravi Shankar was a huge influence on twentieth-century musicians, from pop to classical. He taught many major musicians, from violinist Yehudi Menuhin to pop star George Harrison. Oh, and Shankar also wrote multiple film scores. He broke down barriers, and has set an example for the next generation; his daughter, Anoushka, is herself a sitar player and composer.

Jazzical

Duke Ellington was a famous bandleader, heading up a jazz orchestra for which he wrote pieces of music. He rearranged favourite classical pieces for this ensemble, 'jazzing' up famous works like Pyotr Tchaikovsky's *The Nutcracker Suite* and Edvard Grieg's 'In the Hall of the Mountain King'. Ellington fought against the label of jazz, saying "there's only two kinds of music – good and bad."

73

THE FUTURE OF CLASSICAL

So far, we've looked at the past and present – we've travelled through more than 1,000 years of music!
Where are we headed next?

Streaming

The way we listen to music has changed. Thanks to streaming platforms, music is available to hear at the touch of a button.

It's certainly a long way away from the 1700s, when you might hear your favourite piece of music only once or twice in your entire lifetime!

Playlists

With its use of playlists, streaming can encourage people to listen by mood rather than by genre. There has been a boom in these kinds of classical artists, with 'ambient' tracks designed to provide a soundscape or a certain mood.

Collaboration

The classical world has always been collaborative, like when artist Pablo Picasso painted sets for ballet productions with music by Igor Stravinsky. Today, music has ever-wider collaborations. Italian tenor Andrea Bocelli collaborated with pop star Ed Sheeran on the album *Sì*. Likewise, Gary Barlow collaborated with a full symphony orchestra, Latin groups and jazz quartets for his 2020 album *Music Played By Humans*.

Internationalism

The widespread availability of music means that it's even easier for different cultures and backgrounds to cross-fertilise. One such border-blurring musician is A.R. Rahman from India; he studied Western classical music in London, and has collaborated with everyone from the London Philharmonic Orchestra to Mick Jagger.

Computers and Electronic Sounds

Electronics and computers have changed the way we write music, but also the kind of sounds we can create. Composer Wendy Carlos is celebrated for developing the Moog synthesiser, an electronic keyboard; she has incorporated synthesisers into her film scores.

Similarly, Erland Cooper frequently uses electronics in his music to capture the peace and calm of his native Orkney. His 2018 album *Solan Goose* responds to the claustrophobia of working in a big city like London; it's full of shimmering strings and electronic atmospherics.

Next Generation

There's a fantastic range of young composers emerging onto the classical scene.

Alma Deutscher started playing the piano at the age of two, and wrote a sonata for the instrument at age six. She has a whole album of original piano music out on Sony Classical (*From My Book of Melodies*), which speaks the language of past musical eras and channels the mannerisms of previous composers.

Missy Mazzoli has already been nominated for a Grammy Award. In 2018, she made history as one of the first two women to be commissioned by New York's prestigious Metropolitan Opera. She also writes for the screen, having written and performed music for the Amazon TV programme *Mozart in the Jungle*.

FIND OUT MORE

From my own career, one thing is clear: there are lots of great organisations, orchestras, charities and outlets supporting young musicians. Classical music is not an ivory tower or a distant bubble: we welcome new listeners and want you involved! Here are some groups particularly worth exploring if you want to find out more...

UK charities and organisations

🎵 **Music for Youth:** a national UK charity that gives a stage to more than 60,000 young people every year, across all music genres. It puts on concerts at top venues like the Royal Albert Hall and Birmingham Symphony Hall. Every young person who performs gets feedback from a professional music mentor. All events are free to take part in. www.mfy.org.uk

🎵 **Orchestras for All:** this UK charity runs a national orchestra of 100 for 11–18-year-olds, while their Modulo Programme helps provide music resources to schools and creates regional pop-up orchestras. www.orchestrasforall.org

🎵 **Youth Music:** this national UK charity provides money to help music projects for young people aged 0–25. It funds 300 projects every year, supporting 83,000 young people. www.youthmusic.org.uk

🎵 **Music in Secondary Schools Trust:** this charity was set up by a headteacher and provides musical instruments and lessons to schools. It is supported by the legendary musicals composer and producer Andrew Lloyd Webber. www.misst.org.uk

🎵 **Music Masters:** "Every child deserves a great music education." This charity hosts workshops with top classical musicians in schools. www.musicmasters.org.uk

🎵 **Orchestras Live:** this organisation believes orchestras should be for everyone, and work with all age ranges. It helps 15,000 young people every year, with opportunities to work with ensembles. It hosts lullaby concerts for 20,000 young people and families, offering an introduction to classical music. www.orchestraslive. org.uk/inspiring-children-and-young-people

UK Radio Stations and Podcasts

♫ **Magic Radio's Magic Classical (formerly Scala Radio):** launched in March 2019, this plays music ranging from classical favourites through to the latest videogame score, as well as classical arrangements of pop songs. My programme, the *Culture Bunker*, has gone behind the scenes in classical music, meeting the people who do the work, with guests including pop star Gary Barlow, violinist and conductor Itzhak Perlman and soprano Renée Fleming. It celebrates all music and musicians on an even field: everyone and everything is welcome.

♫ **Classic FM:** launched in 1992, this station provides long stretches of familiar classical favourites, with presenters from the world of news, media and music.

♫ **BBC Radio 3:** the UK's oldest classical radio station, today it is home to world music and jazz, as well as regular informative shows like *Composer of the Week* (exploring one great composer each week), and *Record Review* (celebrating great recordings). Radio 3 also broadcasts every concert in the annual summer festival of classical music, the BBC Proms, and highlights the latest young talent with their New Generation Artists scheme.

♫ **Sticky Notes: The Classical Music Podcast:** introduces key works and ideas, featuring interviews with contemporary legends like jazz/classical trumpeter Wynton Marsalis and composer Gabriela Lena Frank.

Magazines and Websites

♫ **Gramophone:** established in 1923, this magazine is celebrated for its comprehensive reviews of the latest classical recordings. Its website features a handy guide to the top composers. www.gramophone.co.uk

♫ **BBC Music Magazine:** a publication with a website to explore, including topical articles, interviews and profiles. www.classical-music.com

♫ **English National Opera:** an opera company that sings all productions in English (when many operas are sung in Italian or German, if originally written in that language). The ENO also has a handy introduction to opera on their website: www.eno.org/discover-opera

Streaming Platforms

There are so many great platforms to sample classical music and create your own playlists. Here are just a few:

♫ **Apple Music Classical:** a dedicated app that's designed specifically for classical music.

♫ **Idagio:** a specialised streaming service, with both free and paid tiers.

♫ **Presto:** a classical and jazz streaming service.

♫ **Spotify:** a digital music, podcast and video service.

♫ **YouTube Music:** a music service with official albums, singles, videos, remixes, live performances and more.